VERANDA

INSPIRED BY
COLOR

VERANDA

INSPIRED BY
COLOR

CLINTON SMITH

HEARST
books

Though a working knowledge of the color wheel is a key component of an artist's toolbox, so much of how interior designers use color is innate. These homes from the pages of *Veranda* demonstrate a poetic mastery of radiant hues, be it an instinctive sense of the just-right shade, a gutsy gamble on an oddball pairing, or the knack for an intentional mismatch.

In alluring palettes, the houses collected here hum with emotion. They harness color in ways both shocking and sublime. There are rooms that invigorate, rooms that delight and inspire, and rooms that comfort and cosset. But most important, these rooms tell stories. At its heart, color is deeply personal—a pure expression of self writ large in the walls, floors, fabrics, and even ceilings of a home. More than a backdrop, color is a declaration of intention: It sets the tone for how you want to live. It is the embodiment of who you are and what you find beautiful.

—CLINTON SMITH

Pretty&

Comforting

Never underestimate the power of pretty. Though it can be easy to dismiss in a world that favors the bold and the new, there's an enduring, bright-eyed beauty found in soft textiles, romantic florals, and cheery checks and stripes. When everyone's in such a rush, there's nothing more refreshing than welcoming, gracious rooms that beg us to slow down. These homes are gifts: crisp accents, classic shapes, thoughtful details, and a touch of wild whimsy, all wrapped in a graceful package and topped with a glamorous bow. Revel in just-right bright hues—some delicate, some daring—that seem to be chosen with the express purpose of inviting in the sunshine and inspiring joy. The secret is that there's nothing simple at all about pretty—but pretty feels, quite simply, divine.

ISLAND IDYLL A summer retreat passed down for generations goes from formal to family-friendly without sacrificing an ounce of style.

A proponent of old-fashioned decorating in luscious hues, Los Angeles-based decorator Ruthie Sommers is known for rooms that are modern in spirit but have a sense of the past. In Newport, Rhode Island, she helped third-generation homeowners put their stamp on the family summer home they had recently inherited—transforming prim rooms into warm, welcoming spaces without trampling on tradition.

Pops of pink set the stage for a bright, joyous home brimming with personality and charm—from the trim of the main staircase's stately navy runner to a pair of plush fuchsia armchairs that warm up the ice-blue living room. "A colorful room really gives you the feeling that you can put your feet up," says designer Ruthie Sommers. "This is a place where you'd hang out with girlfriends, or spend a lazy Sunday, or where kids can play."

Many of the rooms are inspired riffs on family heirlooms. In the library, Sommers kept the wood-paneled walls and a cream sofa covered in a delicate celadon-and-lavender pattern. She amped up the purples and greens throughout the room—a violet club chair and geometric rug, vibrant stools with a tiger stripe—then added orange velvet curtains that feel irreverent and youthful. "The house works so well in part because it's not perfectly matched," says Sommers. "It wasn't all 'out with the old, in with the new.' I wanted to make it feel like it had evolved, instead."

13

OPPOSITE PAGE: *Pink trim gives the navy menswear-inspired runner a playful edge.* FOLLOWING PAGES: *Sommers deploys tropical prints and fuchsia accents to bring lightness and levity to the living room.*

THIS PAGE: *The formal wood-paneled study gets a youthful update with chartreuse tiger-stripe upholstery and orange accents.* OPPOSITE PAGE: *Even the silk lampshades get a dash of color in a bright corner; the jade banquette provides an extra perch for entertaining and showcases an antique screen.*

OPPOSITE PAGE: *In the butler's pantry, cobalt blue lacquered cabinetry brings high style to a utilitarian room.*
THIS PAGE: *The red-and-white kitchen features a geometric painted floor, playful prints, and pops of blue.*

"Everyone wants to talk about the color that's hot right now, but for me color is never just another trend. It's ebullient, endless, boundless. When you walk into a colorful room, you smile. I love to add color to unexpected, underutilized nooks and hallways— the unsung heroes of the house—to make you want to transition through those spaces." —Ruthie Sommers

THIS PAGE: *Sweet violet wallpaper in the master bath leads into a closet that's a riot of electric purples and limes, complete with a citron-hued floor.* OPPOSITE PAGE: *The master bedroom's butter-yellow paneled walls were a holdover from the homeowners' grandparents.*

FOR THE LOVE OF CHIC A Chicago family's urbane townhouse reflects an irreverent devotion to all things dashing and brilliant.

In a Lincoln Park townhome she designed for a young family, Ruthie Sommers took her cues from her clients, who were looking for bold colors that would counteract Chicago's dreary winter days. "This family is active, playful, and fun," says Sommers, "and that's exactly how their home reads."

She swathed the dining area in glorious panoramic wallpaper depicting scenes of old India in grisaille, blown up in scale for a modern look; two-tone green dining chairs with embroidered medallions add to the festive air. In a stairwell nook, dark purple lacquered walls and upholstered doors bring unexpected glamour to a space others might be prone to overlook. Even in the home's the most subdued, tonic space, Sommers still packs a punch: The living room is quietly voluptuous, laced with prim touches like a pink velvet sofa scalloped like a seashell and ladylike pinch-pleat curtains in the same soft taupe as the silk walls.

And for all of the saturated hues, Sommers created spaces that may soften over time. "Everything we did was malleable," she says. "In each room, there's one robust element that's easily replaceable." Swap the family room's purple sofa or those peridot dining chairs for cream upholstery and the rooms would take on an entirely different tenor. "They can always change those bright hues," says Sommers, "and by leaving that possibility open, I think they'll enjoy them even more while they have them."

OPPOSITE PAGE: *Lacquered eggplant walls and upholstered doors brighten a basement stairwell nook.*

THIS PAGE: *A sky blue ceiling strikes a cheery note in the subdued salon-style living room.*
OPPOSITE PAGE: *The dining room's exotic embellishments channel Doris Duke's Shangri La.*

THIS PAGE: *The family room's walls are clad in a sunny linen print.*
OPPOSITE PAGE: *A pleated sunburst canopy gilds a daughter's bed.*

HAUTE HUES Two sisters balance the grandeur of a Dallas house with an unabashed passion for color.

A lot is asked of the Dallas house that designer Kelli Ford shares with her husband and their two daughters. It must be grand enough to accommodate a hundred dressed-up guests for cocktails on a Friday night, kid-friendly enough to host a gaggle of second-graders at a Saturday afternoon pool party, and cozy enough to serve as a spot where the Fords can kick back on a Sunday to watch a Cowboys game. With that in mind, Ford—who worked on the house with her sister and business partner, Kirsten Fitzgibbons—used classical touches, bold colors, and exuberant patterns to strike a balance between formal elegance and whimsy.

Both designers are drawn to evocative color. Because her husband's favorite is yellow, Ford gave him a brilliant version that approaches pure primary pigment for the art-lined gallery. (It also reappears as a vibrant accent chair in the chocolate-hued master bedroom.) Blue, though, occupies a special place in the sisters' hearts. There's the summer-afternoon azure in the office's vaulted ceiling, a diffuse, almost foggy hue lacquered in her master bath, and a dazzling family room done up in a medley of blue-and-white prints from floor to ceiling. "There are too many white and beige rooms out there," says Ford. "I like them, but I think one can be more daring—it pays off."

29

OPPOSITE PAGE: *The geometry of the gallery's geometric stone floor—inspired by the work of the late David Hicks— tempers the exuberance of the egg yolk–colored walls.* FOLLOWING PAGES: *Custom periwinkle wall panels are embellished with gold leaf.*

THIS PAGE: *Exuberant pattern enlivens a mahogany paneled room.*
OPPOSITE PAGE: *Chandeliers embellished with purple rock crystal match the walls of the dining room, which were meticulously hand-painted to look like ikat fabric.*

"I balance bright rooms with light, airy ones. The most important thing is to have a flow—bringing a color that was predominant in one room into the room adjoining it, even just as a couple of pillows, to create a connection." —Kelli Ford

35

ENDLESS SUMMER The radiant colors of the sea enliven a family's vacation home at the shore.

For years, Kelli Ford's family has decamped from Dallas to their oceanside home in Southampton for the summer. And for more than a decade, they had admired the five-bedroom house across the street, on Shinnecock Bay. So when the property came up for sale, the Fords looked to the future. "It's a getaway from our getaway," says Ford. "We wanted a place that would lure our girls back after they are grown and gone,"

The previous owner, the celebrated tastemaker Carolyne Roehm, had gutted the house and recast it in blue and white, lining the living room from floor to ceiling in delft tile and turning the master bathroom into a mini hammam. For most decorators embarking on a new project, the impulse is to start fresh. But for Ford and Fitzgibbons—both noted blue-and-white enthusiasts—seeing the interior for the first time was like coming home.

While the pair felt no need to tear the place apart, they did want to put their own spin on it. Energizing the rooms was easy for this sister act, whose exuberant sense of color and pattern flows through the house like the water that rushes beneath it at high tide. They appointed bold checks, exotic ikats, French stripes, lavish florals, and elaborate chinoiserie with such a sense of timelessness that it's doubtful Ford's daughters will ever want to change a thing.

OPPOSITE PAGE: *Grape linen walls are a bright backdrop for a guest room's exuberant floral upholstery.*
FOLLOWING PAGES: *The living room's color scheme was designed to coordinate with the existing delft tiles.*

OPPOSITE PAGE: *Floor-to-ceiling tiles in a rich azure create a jewel-box effect in the master bath.*
THIS PAGE: *The mahogany shiplap paneling on the upstairs landing recalls the interior of a luxury ocean liner—the only nautical reference in sight—and offers a view of colorful guest rooms decked in ebullient florals.* FOLLOWING PAGES: *Blue-and-white striped cushions adorn chaises on the expansive deck.*

NATURAL INSTINCT In her own Dallas townhome, Jan Showers deploys subtle island-inspired hues with timeless grace.

Though her vacation to St. Barts with her husband was supposed to be a break from design work, "all I was doing was thinking about colors," says decorator Jan Showers. Inspiration abounded in the serene landscape—sandy beaches, bright sky, shimmering waves. By the time they returned to Dallas, she had settled on a palette: a soothing sea of not-quite neutrals, all in similar values. "There are no dramatic shifts to very light or very dark hues," she says, "but that doesn't mean there's no drama."

Showers painted the living room a pale chameleon-like hue that feels gray during the day but reads as a pale blue by lamplight at night. A pieced cowhide rug and soft beige upholstery lend a cozy touch, while a custom mirrored fireplace surround and screen lend a reflective glow. To offset the vastness of the high-ceilinged room, she hung a chandelier lower than usual, creating the illusion of a more intimate space. In her office, she softened the effects of soaring ceilings with a warm tan paint ("cozy like a vicuna coat," she says), while the bedroom's parrot-green bed hangings are a striking nod to the room's verticality.

The home feels so fresh, it's a surprise to learn that it has remained largely unchanged for more than a decade—a true testament to her unerring eye. "Good design is always good," she says. "I don't like trends, so I'm in better shape to not have rooms that look dated."

OPPOSITE PAGE: *A custom fireplace surround and screen are made of antiqued mirror; above the fireplace, the artwork is painted on a mirrored surface for extra shimmer.* FOLLOWING PAGES: *The high-ceilinged living room strikes a contemporary yet cozy note decked in effervescent champagne hues.*

OPPOSITE PAGE: *Separate seating areas make the large living room feel intimate; geometric pillows add a subtle shot of color.* **THIS PAGE:** *The dining room's cool blue, inspired by the water in St. Barts, is also the perfect backdrop for art.* **FOLLOWING PAGES:** *Against aubergine walls, the master bedroom's parrot-green canopy brings extra drama.*

55

OPPOSITE PAGE: *In a warm toffee hue, the office's sitting area is endlessly inviting.*
THIS PAGE: *Amethyst and fuchsia accents are an elegant counterpoint to the neutral furnishings.*

EASY DOES IT
Amanda Nisbet imagines a colorful weekend house in the Hamptons that is footloose, friendly, and fun.

As summer rolls around, a busy New York City family of five migrates to their gracious, sun-swept home on the bay in the quiet Hamptons town of Quogue. Sailboats drift lazily in the distance, and everyone shifts into a blessedly lower gear. The homeowners each came from big, boisterous families, so their seemingly endless supply of bedrooms is filled with family and friends. The vibe is cozy and casual: barefoot guests, frosty beverages, and fresh fish on the grill.

The setting is unmistakably beachy but free of seaside clichés. In the hands of designer Amanda Nisbet, a sense of bayside calm is achieved through her signature combination of classic shapes, lively patterns, and pops of bright colors set against wide-open spaces sheathed in whites and creams. She deftly combines any number of bold hues—some of which might be expected to clash but that in her hands flow seamlessly together. In a high-ceilinged family room, dusty pinks give way to beige wainscoting, and chartreuse meets periwinkle in a guest bedroom that's surprisingly serene. Classic blue-and-white abounds as well, but always with a twist—like sleek navy-lacquered cabinetry in the butler's pantry or the undulating living room rug designed to suggest the sea. "It's important to acknowledge where you are, in this case a beach house," says Nisbet, "but that doesn't mean giving in to tired notions."

57

OPPOSITE PAGE: *Bright accents and free-form patterns enliven a traditional dining room.*
FOLLOWING PAGES: *With its watery hues, the living room nods to tradition but feels fresh and modern.*

THIS PAGE: *Nisbet's attention to detail extends to the embellished mauve trim along the curves of an armchair.* OPPOSITE PAGE: *A white lantern made of shells suspended in the butler's pantry stands out against the navy-lacquered cabinetry and sterling accents.* FOLLOWING PAGES: *A dramatic upholstered headboard is the focal point in a citron guest bedroom.*

A DELFT TOUCH Cathy Kincaid blanketed a Dallas home in soft blues and whites, inspired by her client's lifelong collection of porcelain.

When the pretty 1930s Spanish Colonial across the street went on the market, Dallas designer Cathy Kincaid's clients leapt at the chance to restore the home to its former glory. Though originally from the East Coast, they had spent more than twenty years in Santa Barbara before moving to Dallas, so they were well-acquainted with the charms of its intimate rooms and Moorish touches. "You feel comfortable in these spaces," says the wife. "The proportions, the ceiling height—they are attuned to the human scale."

Inside, Kincaid furnished the home in a medley of blue-and-white patterns and prints. Barely there hues create a neutral shell, while antique textiles and painted furniture impart recurring red, pale violet, and gold accents that feel gentle and worn-in rather than bright and crisp. (Only in the library, a cozy space where the couple spend there evenings reading by the fire, do the enveloping cantaloupe-lacquered walls and olive curtains depart from the all-blue scheme.) The effect is most profound in the dining room, with its platters and vases on the walls and antique Portuguese tiles for wainscoting. "It's porcelain overload— almost as though the walls were papered with plates," admits Kincaid. Rather than retreat, she doubled down on delicate patterns with embellished curtains and upholstery. "It all works because the colors and the scale of the patterns talk to each other rather than collide," she says. "Sometimes, the more you add, the less busy it seems."

65

OPPOSITE PAGE: *A Dallas dining room was designed to complement a collection of blue-and-white porcelain.*

THIS PAGE: *An antique French canvas screen, chinoiserie-upholstered club chairs, and antique textiles on the sofa's pillows add red accents to the blue-and-white living room.* OPPOSITE PAGE: *The breakfast room was designed to highlight a mustard-hued porcelain collection.* FOLLOWING PAGES: *A lacquer finish—cantaloupe on the walls and a coral ceiling—creates a warm glow in the library and reflects the flicker of the fireplace at night.*

THIS PAGE: *Two-tone geometric tiles give the sunroom a modern edge.* OPPOSITE PAGE: *A hot tub and cold plunge pool in the spa are framed by elegant stripes and Greek key tile.*

HIGH VOLTAGE Alessandra Branca energizes a Chicago townhouse with a confident mix that bridges the best of old and new.

In a 19th-century Chicago townhome, sheathed by its former owners in a sea of Sheetrock, one couple saw, if not beauty, limitless potential. Their secret weapon was decorator Alessandra Branca, known for her reverence for a home's history, who agreed to help them restore the space to its former glory. Up came the standard-issue maple floors, and down went French maple in a chevron pattern, wire-brushed and coated in beeswax to look like it had been there all along. Ceilings were coved, fireplaces mounted, a winding banister erected, and moldings added to define the comfortable proportions of the rooms. She even clad the living room walls in parchment pieces cut to look like blocks of marble.

Branca's gift for transformation went far beyond the architecture; her love for playing with textures and finishes shows up throughout the house. She harnessed color, form, and scale to create captivating rooms notable for their insouciant mix of periods and styles: A Damien Hirst print inspired a kaleidoscopic mix of patterns in the living room, where a pair of early Empire floor lamps got a sleek, chic treatment with a sleeve of glass and hot-pink silk shades from Thailand; elsewhere, she covered Gustavian dining chairs in white leather for a modern update. "By allowing me to play—with art, architecture, materials, surfaces, geometry, color—my clients let me bring life into every room," says Branca.

OPPOSITE PAGE: *Branca cranks up the drama with lacquered walls at the entrance to the master bedroom for a high-contrast look.* FOLLOWING PAGES: *Pieces in an array of styles and materials feel in sync in a unified palette; on a pair of modern armchairs, a classic fabric in electric purple is surprising and fresh.*

THIS PAGE: *In the dining room, European antiques mingle effortlessly with shapely modern pieces.* OPPOSITE PAGE: *Dark high-gloss trim brings crisp detail to the lounge.*

THIS PAGE: *A bright avocado hue enlivens a classically furnished guest bedroom.* **OPPOSITE PAGE:** *Organic hand-painted wallpaper in crisp navy and white is a striking twist on a traditional pattern.*

ABSINTHE AQUA
BLUSH BOUGAINV
BURGUNDY BUTT
CARDINAL CELE
COCOA CORAL CO
DAFFODIL DELE
FLAMINGO FUCH
IRIS KEY LIME
MARBLE MARI
NAVY PEACH PE
PIMENTO PISTA
VERDIGRIS WH

MARINE AZURE
ILLEA BOXWOOD
ER CANTALOUPE
RY CLEMENTINE
RNFLOWER CYAN
T EUCALYPTUS
SIA GERANIUM
LEMON LILAC
GOLD MAUVE
NY PINEAPPLE
CHIO VERBENA
EATWISTERIA

Earthy &

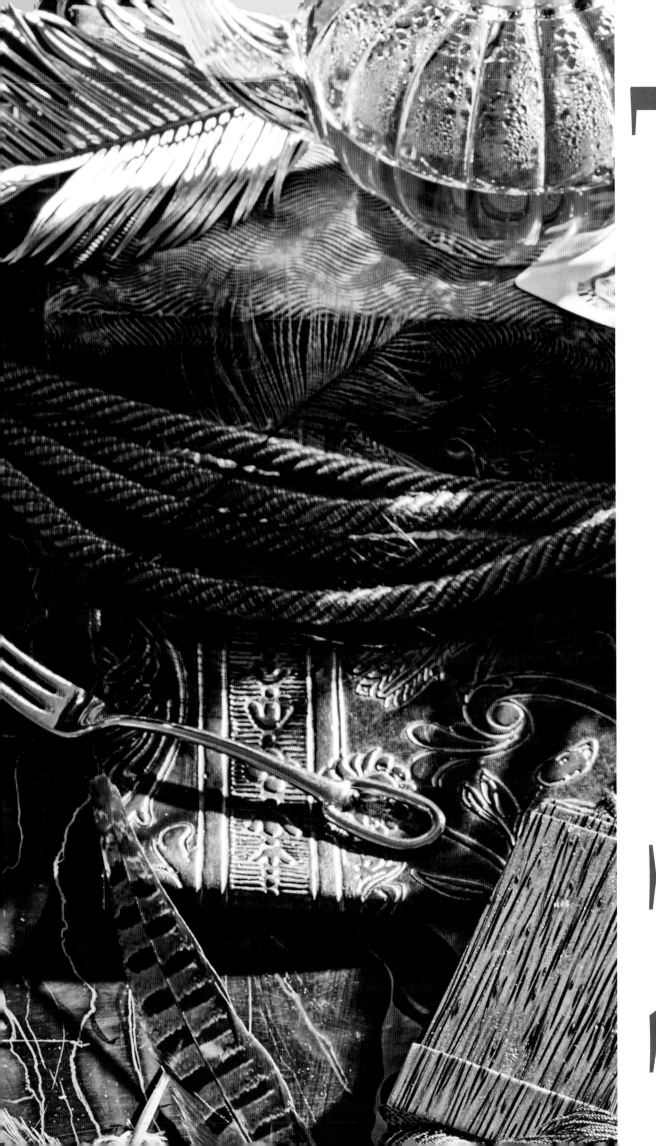

Natural

The lure of the land is undeniable. So, too, is the arresting quality of rooms that harness the beauty and bounty of the landscape. Whether ripe with drama or traditional and tucked-in, the inherent mystery and sense of wonder the outdoors inspires is not lost in translation: Imbued with depth and dimension, these spaces accentuate the exuberance of the natural world, then recast it in human scale to bring it inside—a cool, cloudy violet mountaintop haze, a sun-drenched desert panorama, and the moody, evocative shimmer of a roiling sea, all reimagined in lush, luxurious homes. It's worth marveling at how something so sublime can also be so of the earth—and yet it's no wonder we feel so at home.

MAGICAL MOOD In her Atlanta home, Susan Ferrier crafts an atmosphere of intrigue and wonder, creating a veritable cabinet of curiosities.

Designer Susan Ferrier's rooms are the visual equivalent of a Gregorian chant: dusky and glinting, tranquil and exciting. Her slipcovers even evoke the simplicity of monks' robes. Bright color is banished—she'd rather play with extremes of light and dark. Small furnishings are kept out—she's more interested in the mysteries of exaggerated scale. And though she gravitates towards shapes that feel sleekly modern, her accessories include architectural fragments recalling the past.

When Ferrier and her husband bought their home—a 1920s Tudor sited on nearly an acre in Druid Hills, the historic Frederick Law Olmsted–designed neighborhood in Atlanta—it was an abandoned wreck. A thorough renovation transformed the house into the perfect backdrop for Ferrier's evocative, large-scale decorating. In the living room, the moldings were removed to emphasize the sculptural furnishings; the updated kitchen features striking black cabinets and ebonized black floors. The smoky, soulful palette of gray, slate, and washed-out shades of beige and olive, trimmed with burnished metallic accents, continues throughout the house. It all adds up to a cohesive atmosphere—a trance, really—that's as sensuous and velvety soft as it is dramatic. "I'm not afraid of power and strength," says Ferrier. "I want to make rooms that hold you and make you feel safe, that you don't slip through."

OPPOSITE PAGE: *Ferrier's evocative furnishings create a moody tableau.* FOLLOWING PAGES: *Shapely pieces in a sea of cloudy hues lend a sensual, enveloping air to the living room—Ferrier even removed moldings throughout the house to emphasize the sculptural furnishings.*

THIS PAGE: *A vintage ornament converted into a light fixture adds breathtaking scale to the dining room.*
OPPOSITE PAGE: *The library is filled with lush teal touches and an eclectic mix of one-of-a-kind wonders.*

"The secret to getting any room right is the light: I don't select a single finish or fabric without setting it out and letting the natural light rest on it. Using metallics is my way of playing with the lighting, with reflectivity. When placed correctly, those pieces make your eye move through the room." — Susan Ferrier

OPPOSITE PAGE: *The breakfast nook is a master class in using texture to create variety in a neutral room.*
THIS PAGE: *The kitchen features striking black cabinets and ebonized floors.*

OPPOSITE PAGE: *In the master bedroom, thirteen-foot-high bed curtains in an earthy olive hue accentuate an opulent headboard.* **THIS PAGE:** *Ferrier created a still life of stacked suitcases, while a pair of worn French chairs wear their original teal velvet.*

A SOFT TOUCH   In glamorous spin on coastal style, a Florida beach house shimmers with glamorous details and dreamy hues.

The simple white stucco exterior of the beachfront manse concocted by architect Bobby McAlpine and designer Susan Ferrier at Alys Beach on the Florida panhandle belies the glittering furnishings inside. Designed for a Birmingham family of six, the house itself is a highly polished shell: "handsome but unfussy, and under-embellished by intention," says McAlpine of the coolly elegant, austere architecture. He took his cues from 1930s Parisian department stores—loftlike rooms with reedy cast-iron columns, mosaic marble floors, and elaborate ceilings—knowing full well that frequent collaborator Ferrier was dreaming of a sumptuous, sparkling interior.

In Ferrier's hands, even hard surfaces like these were made to feel soft and warm in a palette that might as well be fog and starlight. She brought in banks of gauzy drapery and furniture with expressive curves. She laid fluffy white goatskin rugs on top of the polished floors and filled the rooms with muted metallic accents that flicker at night like candlelight. "The mixing of silver and gold is the mantra in this house," says Ferrier. "I've limited the color but amped up the reflectivity." Each piece turns up the volume on romance—sinuous, mirrored, gilded. "Metallics are neutrals for me," she says. "If you don't go crazy with colors, you can go crazy with metallics."

97

OPPOSITE PAGE: *The gilded Swedish daybed is upholstered in a blue that perfectly matches the view of the ocean beyond.*

THIS PAGE: *A palette of gray, white, silver, and gold creates an ethereal mood.* OPPOSITE PAGE: *The dining area's sparkling white mosaic-tiled floor anchors an expansive room, while the open floor plan ensures a dazzling ocean view from every seat.* FOLLOWING PAGES: *Gridded windows overlooking the Gulf of Mexico offer a masculine contrast to the living room's romantic allure.*

THIS PAGE: *Custom cypress paneling creates a restful backdrop in the master bedroom, while the blue accents nod to the bed's ocean view.* OPPOSITE PAGE: *Lounging with sparkle and style is the spa-like master bath's raison d'être.*

PURPLE REIGN In Nashville, Suzanne Kasler turns tradition on its head with a magical, moody color scheme in shades of plum, amethyst, and lavender.

After more than a decade spent abroad in a series of architecturally significant residences—like the 200-year-old Bermudian manse where they lived for a time with three toddlers—designer Suzanne Kasler's clients returned to the States and purchased a stately stone manor in Nashville. Though unfazed by its grand proportions, they sought to infuse a more youthful spirit for their family, with their kids now entering their teens.

"They wanted a foundation of tradition that did not feel traditional," says Kasler. Luckily, combining contemporary motifs with classic ones is her forte. Though she could have stripped away the 1990s-era residence's interior trim to make a series of modernist boxes, she instead did just the opposite, adding flamboyantly ornate moldings to convey the grandeur of an old English country estate. "We wanted to create a history for the house, then make it relevant for today," she explains.

As for the color palette, there are no words to describe it: "Is it lavender or purplish gray?" muses Kasler, struggling to name the shade that infuses the dining room. "More of an eggplant, perhaps?" suggests the wife. Either way, the ethereal color scheme makes the entire house seem serene—from the peaceful master bedroom, with its metallic accents, to the dusty purple-blue hues in the living room. "We've never worked with such indefinable, muted colors before," Kasler says. "But they are so successful here, quiet yet dramatic."

OPPOSITE PAGE: *Watercolor-like grays and blues create an ethereal palette.*

OPPOSITE PAGE: *A small anteroom leading from the first-floor master bedroom into the living room is sheathed in an eye-catching violet.* **THIS PAGE:** *An antique French limestone mantel contrasts with a streamlined sofa in an inky velvet and eye-catching gilded urns.*

OPPOSITE PAGE: *Powdery purples add nuanced color to a neutral palette in the dining room.*
THIS PAGE: *A Gustavian screen in a panoply of hues adds a touch of old-world opulence.*

THIS PAGE: *The master bedroom's elaborately patterned coverlet brings a continental flourish to the room's platinum and steel finishes.* **OPPOSITE PAGE:** *Shimmering Gracie wallpaper transforms a powder room into a teal jewel box.*

PERSONAL BEST An architect creates a new home for himself built specially for a lifetime's worth of cherished collections.

In the leafy Birmingham community of Mountain Brook, architect James Carter designed and built his "forever" house. Simple and elegant, formal but a bit rambling, the brick Georgian looks as though it might have grown up from the space ages ago. That same easy grace permeates the interiors, too: warm, welcoming rooms decked in robust hues derived from the English textiles used liberally throughout. "I didn't want a neutral house," says Carter. "All of the historic homes in Ireland, Italy, Charleston, and New England that I've admired—none of them were white." He clad the library in stained wood, while hallways and guest rooms are covered in traditional stripes and delicate florals that pair seamlessly with his collection of English Regency furniture and American antiques.

To help with the mix, Carter enlisted his close friend Jane Hawkins Hoke, a designer and longtime collaborator whom he calls his "safety net and guiding spirit." When he wanted to paint the octagonal dining room's walls a bright burnt orange, his favorite color, she talked him into apricot instead—which he conceded, albeit in high gloss. She also pushed him towards the vibrant green in the master bedroom. "So many people love it but say they wouldn't have the guts to do it," says Carter of the bold hue. "I think people who are comfortable with themselves are comfortable with color. It's like a woman in a rust-colored dress at a party where everyone's wearing black—I'm going to talk to her first."

OPPOSITE PAGE: *The apricot octagonal dining room was sized and colored to set off an antique Italian screen; built-in bookshelves, green-gray trim, and plainspoken bare floors lend rustic charm to the classic furnishings.*
FOLLOWING PAGES: *Antique oak paneling gives this Birmingham library a warm, weathered look.*

THIS PAGE: *Architectural drawings are hung salon-style on a gold stripe in the halls of the house.*
OPPOSITE PAGE: *Gold accents and charming floral fabrics in mustard and rust hues enliven
a sweet nook in a guest bedroom.*

THIS PAGE: *In an enveloping green, the master bedroom is at once intimate and grand; Carter calls the foliage-inspired color "strong and cozy."* **OPPOSITE PAGE:** *Carter especially loves the way the bedroom's green walls provide a striking backdrop for his collection of gouaches.*

DESERT ROSE A romantic by nature and a classicist by choice, John Saladino brings his unique sensibility to a house near Palm Springs.

On his first site visit to a client's home in Palm Springs, designer John Saladino looked out the window for inspiration: "I saw the colors of the light on the desert stones and the mountains, and said, 'There's the palette right there,' he recalls. The homeowners —a couple who winter in the Spanish-style house, and who had fallen for its seductive views of the Santa Rosa Mountains and its hiking access to the Mount San Jacinto wilderness— embraced his thirst for a vibrant interpretation of the landscape they loved.

The resulting interior is an unexpected blend of pinks, cream, mustard yellows, and magenta. "These are extremely unusual colors to use together in a living room," says Saladino. "If this were foggy Scotland, it would look lurid, but I knew that here the desert light would extract some if its intensity and power." A rosy hue used for slipcovers and upholstery on chairs and sofas echoes the bougainvillea on the property and the deep pink that haloes the mountains around sunset. The mustard that crops up on throw pillows, passementeries, and antique fauteuils comes from a native blossom.

Throughout the home, the designer savors the dramatic tension achieved through juxtaposition: baroque with modern, primitive with refined, explicit with implied. "I edit constantly because what you omit or hold back is just as important as what you include," he says. "But all of my work aside, in this house the desert mountains are the main performance."

OPPOSITE PAGE: *The stone-clad entry conforms to the arid brown tones of the desertscape.* **FOLLOWING PAGES:** *The large living room was painted a rosy taupe and divided into three seating areas; amaranth-pink upholstery and goldenrod-hued pillows are a vibrant interpretation of the landscape at sunset.*

"I seek serenity—subtle colors that are appropriate for creating repose, like the palest shade of celadon or a whisper of soft blue. And I always favor texture over pattern, which can be so trendy. A plain color will never betray you—it's a background that allows for change: Table settings change, flowers change according to the season, people change their clothing. Even people add color to a room." —John Saladino

PRECEDING PAGES: *A dining area cloaked in dusty periwinkle creates a cool retreat from the desert sun.*
OPPOSITE PAGE: *Open or closed, the loggia curtains change the mood of the outdoor patio.* THIS PAGE: *In stately browns and shades of pale blue, a formal sitting room is awash in arid tones.* FOLLOWING PAGES: *Dressed entirely in warm indigo hues, a guest room inspires rest and relaxation.*

SALADINO IN SOHO In Manhatta's trendy SoHo neighborhood, the Vermeer painting *Girl with a Pearl Earring* inspired a *Veranda* show house in a modern condominium.

As one of the great Dutch painters of the 17th century, Johannes Vermeer transformed scenes of everyday life into masterpieces revered for their silent intensity, purity of light, and form. Similarly, in a *Veranda* show house, John Saladino's mastery of light, color, and scale lend themselves to the same exultations. "It was easy for me to see that the Vermeer references would work with what I believe makes beautiful interiors," says Saladino. "I bring the attitude of a fine artist to my work. Every room is a walk-in still life."

To re-create the quiet, intimate mood of Vermeer's paintings, Saladino used a soft, neutral palette of creamy whites, deep taupes, and rich pewter with carefully orchestrated lavender and periwinkle-blue accents—some of his favorite colors. Snowy white walls contrast with warm, earthy tones, sumptuous fabrics, and dark leather chairs. The scratch-coat plaster on living-room and breakfast-nook walls mitigates the sterility of the modern architecture and suggests the layering of time.

An ardent theatergoer, Saladino finds inspiration in set design—discreet lighting and backlit sofas and beds are de rigueur in the apartment, and he used mirrors to augment the natural light. "I followed Vermeer's philosophy, which was to take vernacular objects and imbue them with transcendence," he explains. "I wanted to give these rooms an almost ethereal light."

OPPOSITE PAGE: *With a backdrop of earthy scratch-coat plaster, the breakfast nook looks as though it were lifted straight from a still life.* **FOLLOWING PAGES:** *Subtle metal studs and trim are added to periwinkle pillows and upholstery for a modern touch.*

THIS PAGE: *An unconventional dining room, clad in a delicate gray hue, has a soft, ethereal glow.*
OPPOSITE PAGE: *The pewter plates nod to Dutch tradition and provide a refined,*
gleaming counterpoint to the rugged texture of the walls.

APRICOT ASH AU
BITTERSWEET BI
CHARCOAL CLAY C
EVERGREEN FERN
GOLDFINCH HEA
HONEY INDIGO
MOSS MUSTARD
PEACOCK PUCE
PUMPKIN QUINC
RHUBARB ROSE
SANDALWOOD SA
TEAK TURQUOIS

BERGINE BIRCH
BONZE CARAMEL
LOVE COAL CUMIN
FLAX GOLDENROD
THER HIBISCUS
LAPIS LICHEN
OBSIDIAN OLIVE
PUMPERNICKEL
RAISIN RAVEN
RUST SAFFRON
PPHIRE STRAW
TYRIAN ZINNIA

simple &

Pure

White rooms, executed elegantly, are anything but de rigueur. What they lack in kaleidoscopic color, these neutral spaces make up for in heightened drama. They glisten in their austerity. In the simplicity of these homes, there is a quiet, contemplative integrity and a nuanced celebration of texture sheathed in creamy shades. With a palette of all-white hues, the museum-like quality of these spaces shines a spotlight on their furnishings: Distractions stripped away, every piece takes on an elevated responsibility—it must make its mark indelibly against the stark background. They're primed for high contrast, too, with shocking swaths of black, warm wood grains dripping with gilt details, or the sharp edge of modern art to slice through the cloud-like interiors. The effect, of course, is still dreamy.

ARTISTIC AERIE An Atlanta high-rise with sweeping skyline views is the backdrop for a far-ranging collection of extraordinary objects.

As one of the city's top-tier antiques dealers, interior designer Mimi Williams has more than thirty-five years of collecting under her belt—and five storage units filled to the brim. For years, she lived in Atlanta's historic Ansley Park, where she had transformed a Craftsman home into a model of American Federal style—which made her move to a glamorous T-shaped two-bedroom on the forty-second floor of a Buckhead tower all the more surprising. But Williams was looking to downsize, and she jumped when she found the apartment, which features a commanding enfilade of period-style archways running the length of the entry hallway. "I was lucky to find such gorgeous detailing already in place," she says. "It suits me so well."

The all-white apartment presents an elegant foil for the designer's furnishings and art, if only a fraction of it. Hopelessly hooked on travel, Williams has set up her home as a 3-D travelogue, albeit one from a land of neutrals. "I'm known for working in blacks, whites, grays, and naturals," she says. "I like a palette that sets off my things." Those things are an impressive assemblage of 18th-, 19th-, and 20th-century antiques, architectural salvage, and contemporary art. "I've always been fond of cultures colliding," says Williams. "What's more sexy than a well-loved piece of architecture next to a modern painting?"

OPPOSITE PAGE: *A dramatic colonnaded hall with black baseboards bisects the apartment.*

OPPOSITE PAGE: *Williams limits the palette to black and white but mixes pieces from an array of periods and styles with a rich photography collection.* THIS PAGE: *The glass-topped dining table is fashioned from a 19th-century Corinthian capital—a striking contrast to the apartment's modern lines.*

THIS PAGE: *Williams's collection is on full display in the foyer, where she combines a pair of 1940s Frances Elkins loop chairs with a 19th-century goatskin-veneered Italian bar, a set of 10th-century Chinese urns, and art by Mexican, Swedish, and American artists.* OPPOSITE PAGE: *The dining room's open shelving displays a sculptural collection of all-white ceramics.* FOLLOWING PAGES: *The sitting area is dreamy in layered shades of creamy neutrals. Williams left the handsome casement windows curtainless so as not to detract from the apartment's striking 360-degree city views.*

SURPRISE PACKAGE Kay Douglass says "so long" to dark rooms, crystal chandeliers, and billowing valances in favor of airy, light-filled spaces where timeless architecture can shine.

Behind the facade of her 1930s Georgian Revival, Atlanta designer Kay Douglass's rooms are stripped to the essentials. A succession of thoughtful owners had preserved the home's pilasters, theatrical dentils, and multipaned windows—all details that reminded Douglass of the welcoming lounge in Belgium's glorious Hotel Julien, which is carved from two lavish 16th-century buildings in the center of old Antwerp. "The furniture is modern and spare, but you're surrounded by all this ornate Baroque architecture," she explains. "It's one of the prettiest places I've ever been, and it is always on my mind."

Cool white walls and floors in a pure gray set the stage for Douglass's restrained aesthetic. In the living room, the simple contrast of shapely slipcovered sofas next to boxy, velvet-upholstered armchairs creates drama; the windows are left bare and the mantel is devoid of art so that the room's stately moldings stand out in graphic relief. In the master bedroom, a voluptuous French mirror is all that's needed for maximum glamour. "I live an edited lifestyle," she explains. "It's as much about what I don't put into a room as what I do. Adding things for the sake of adding them doesn't make sense to me." Within that restrained shell, color pulses into the house in staccato, single-shot bursts, doled out on scene-stealing twenty-four-inch square pillows. "They're like candy—very tempting," Douglass admits. "An array of them inspires me so much more than pattern."

151

OPPOSITE PAGE: *Hot-pink throw pillows and modern art provide a shot of color in a dramatic entryway.*

"White paint isn't the easy way out. It's important to find the right shade of white for a room, depending on the light in the house. Whites all have tints to them—when you lay out a color chart, there's yellow-white and green-white, gray-white and brown-white, even whites with pink or blue undertones. It's really no different than picking the perfect saturated color."—Kay Douglass

153

OPPOSITE PAGE: *In a serene gray envelope, sculptural furnishings animate a spare dining area.*
THIS PAGE: *An informal seating arrangement and turquoise pillows give the living room a modern, unfussy air.*

OPPOSITE PAGE: *A geometric mobile that once hung in the flagship Hermes store in Paris and canary-yellow curtains are modern touches in a dining room featuring an antique farm table.* THIS PAGE: *Pops of yellow and citron enliven a neutral kitchen.* FOLLOWING PAGES: *A lavender upholstered headboard and vivid purple pillows add a serene shot of color in the master bedroom, while ethereal linen curtains pull all the way across the window wall to envelope the space in softness.*

BRIGHT JUST RIGHT Bold choices wake up a 1920s Colonial house in Atlanta with refreshing graphic impact.

"The interior was dark, so our goal was to make it light and bright," says designer Kay Douglass, who worked on the home for a close friend and her family. At the same time, they wanted to honor the pedigree of the Buckhead home, which was built by the Atlanta architect Philip Shutze. "We wanted to lightly modernize the house without doing something inappropriate," she says. A year in the making, the renovation created a refreshing house that's as bold and modern as it is classic and comfortable. Walls were painted subtle shades of off-white and gray, while a rich zinc color creates intimacy in the dining room; the original brown oak floors were lightened with a whitewashed gray paint that echoes the interior's Belgian-influenced undertones.

The serene background allows each room to zing with saturated color. The lively scheme originated in the dining room, with the vibrant kelly-green fabric for the curtains. "It set the tone for the rest of the house," says Douglass of the graphic mix of black, white, and shades of green on the first floor. Upstairs, the master bedroom and the children's rooms are enlivened with bursts of orange and yellow, culminating with the daughter's high-gloss sunflower bathroom. "My clients were skeptical," says Douglass. Even the painters asked, "Are you sure?" But for Douglass, it was an instinctual choice. "I tell clients that it's usually the things they take a chance on that they end up loving the best!"

OPPOSITE PAGE: *Strong shades of green give a historic home cloaked in neutrals a youthful sensibility.*

THIS PAGE: *Gutsy shapes carry minimal, monochromatic décor in the living room. The lime-green mirror walks the line between modern and traditional—a cheeky twist on an old shape.* OPPOSITE PAGE: *The green linen curtains— a powerful juxtaposition against graphite walls—set the tone for pops of color throughout the home's first floor.*

OPPOSITE PAGE: *A whimsical mirror adds a playful note to a child's bathroom.*
THIS PAGE: *Yellow and black accents enliven a serene master bedroom.*

PERFECTLY SUITED After landing in her dream house in a twist of fate, Tara Shaw can't imagine her cherished collection of European antiques living anywhere else.

When her house in New Orleans was being built—for someone else—New Orleans tastemaker Tara Shaw walked by it every day. She loved its severe front, reminiscent of the Haussman-designed facades in Paris, and the wall around the property that seemed to hide a secret courtyard. Although she lived in a charming Victorian at the time, it was French architecture she adored. As Shaw watched the progress, she thought she might want to tackle a similar project someday. "I never dreamed this one would come on the market," she says. When it did, she had to buy it: "It was as though it was built for me."

It certainly seems built to showcase Shaw's collection of furniture, which she describes as "Italian mixed with Swedish, with some French and contemporary." Those pieces, in turn, are mixed with ones from her own line of reproduction furniture, which grew out of her lifelong love of European furnishings. The house is sublimely serene, the space blanketed in her favorite shades of white. "Most of my clients are such busy people, they want to feel their blood pressure drop when they come home," she explains. "That's how I want to feel, too."

OPPOSITE PAGE: *White walls and floors create a spare, gallery-like backdrop for sculptural elements and antiques.* FOLLOWING PAGES: *The dining room floors were painted a custom high-gloss white to give the 18th-century furnishings a fresh look.*

PRECEDING PAGES: *A variety of finishes gives the neutral living room depth and character.* THIS PAGE: *Modern white leather chairs in the breakfast room add a contemporary touch.* OPPOSITE PAGE: *Graphic hand-painted wallpaper and reproduction benches animate a hallway in the master bedroom.*

PRECEDING PAGES: *Amid a collection of stately furniture, the draped white canopy and curtains add a romantic, delicate note to a guest bedroom. Shaw deploys gilt accents throughout the home for a glamorous look.* THIS PAGE: *Ornate carved details add warmth and patina to the monochromatic bath.* OPPOSITE PAGE: *Antique French paneling in Shaw's master bath was refinished in creamy tones for a soft effect.*

SCENES FROM WALL STREET A refined and seductive *Veranda* show house in Manhattan is inspired by two memorable movies.

In a sleek Manhattan apartment, designer Richard Hallberg created a pied-à-terre for the fictional financier Gordon Gekko, played by Michael Douglas in Oliver Stone's two *Wall Street* films. Envisioning a worldly retreat, he assembled disparate elements— an Alexander Calder mobile and sculptural gilt sconces, a raw steel console and a Renaissance line drawing—that, hung together, appear effortlessly stylish. "I love the idea of putting something superrefined against something that may be rough around the edges, but nevertheless well made," he says. "An African basket can have as much integrity as an 18th-century gilt mirror."

In a masculine study—a sexy, mostly black den—walls are covered in a woven black faux leather that catches light and gilded iron étagères that hold unglazed Han pottery; a chalky plaster-slab console is paired with a Dutch-style desk on elaborately turned legs. Throughout the rest of the condo, bright matte-white walls and richly ebonized hardwood floors help make spaces feel cohesive in the just-completed building. The urban sanctum, perched on the fifty-eighth floor of a Fifth Avenue tower, takes in a panorama that stretches from the East River to the Hudson River and beyond, with the Empire State Building looming smack in the middle. Instead of competing, Hallberg created black-and-white spaces—strong but neutral—that allow the gleaming metropolitan architecture to function as part of the décor. "I wasn't trying to turn a modern building into something it wasn't," says Hallberg. "I wanted to respect the clean lines that were already there. Modern backgrounds are a good foil for collections."

177

OPPOSITE PAGE: *An armchair's woven vinyl upholstery adds a heavy dose of texture in a minimalist room.*
FOLLOWING PAGES: *Hallberg uses pieces with traditional shapes in a stark black-and-white palette as a striking backdrop for the Alexander Calder mobile and other contemporary artworks throughout the apartment.*

THIS PAGE: *Sharp lines and bursts of primary colors mix with more organic shapes in the stark white master bedroom.* OPPOSITE PAGE: *Collections from around the world add golden touches.*

OPPOSITE PAGE: *A textured black wall covering flips the script and provides a striking backdrop for a sculptural white console.* THIS PAGE: *A pieced hide rug brightens the dark, sexy study.*

CAPITAL IDEA Just beyond Washington, D.C., the legendary Marwood Estate enters the 21st century.

The thirty-room residence on the outskirts of the capital is a local legend, a château on the Potomac River that has hosted four U.S. presidents for dinner. The house's facade— modeled in part on Malmaison, Napoleon and Josephine's 18th-century mansion just outside of Paris—had weathered the decades just fine. It's interior, though, was another matter. "It required four years to restore the grandness of the original vision and to bring it up to date," says designer Mary Douglas Drysdale, who spearheaded the renovation.

A fifteen-foot-wide central hallway bisects the home's first floor from front to back. On one side, Drysdale decorated the rooms in a more classical style; on the other, she used a lighter touch for a relaxed family atmosphere. Throughout, the spaces are glazed in creamy tones and fine millwork to create a consistent soft patina; statuesque curtains in soothing shades emphasize the height of the superbly proportioned rooms and frame a picturesque curve in the river. Drysdale adorned floors and new cornice moldings with Greek key borders, stars, medallions, and other neoclassical motifs, which reappear in custom embroidery on upholstery and pillows, "echoing the architecture, but reinterpreted to feel modern." The estate is furnished with French antiques and custom-designed pieces that reiterate the structure's neoclassical lines. Amid such traditional elements, contemporary art provides a bold contrast—a fresh, energizing jolt. "I wanted formality and informality," says Drysdale. "Today, we expect that even the grandest rooms be approachable and comfortable."

OPPOSITE PAGE: *Modern art adds vitality to a traditional setting, while painted furniture and soft yellow fabrics add a delicate dose of color.* FOLLOWING PAGES: *Shades of pale celadon suffuse a stately sitting room; the simple linen of the valences softens the formality of the architecture.*

THIS PAGE: *In the entry, new boiserie blends with freshly mined French limestone for the floor tiles, which were cut on the diagonal and tumbled for a worn look.* OPPOSITE PAGE: *Gilded elements, including custom embroidery that echoes the architecture's neoclassical motifs, stand out in an all-white room.* FOLLOWING PAGES: *The master bedroom's pale blue trim even makes a cameo as a thin ribbon of painted color on the creamy paneling; the custom bed, tucked into an upholstered niche, feels gently enveloping.*

THIS PAGE: *In a subdued palette, the master bath is a serene retreat.*
OPPOSITE PAGE: *A graphic mirror over a sculptural tub illustrates the power of simplicity.*

GUSTAVIAN DELIGHT A tranquil apartment melds a love of Swedish style with a finely tuned modern perspective.

As a child, a San Francisco real estate agent spent idyllic summers near Stockholm, playing in the historic lakeside gardens of Haga Park. There, she discovered Gustav III's Pavilion, a neoclassical royal party palace with mirrored rooms and petite salons rendered in an unforgettable color palette of periwinkle, gold, and chalky white. So when she acquired a sunstruck apartment perched atop one of San Francisco's highest hills, she turned to interior designer Greg Stewart, a principal at ODADA, with the pavilion's timeless beauty and feeling of tranquility as her inspiration.

To start, Stewart outfitted the apartment's interiors with lacquered wall panels and glass floor tiles, both in crisp white, and polished stainless steel on all of the baseboards and window frames. Within that sleek shell, he created a perfect modern rendition of the pavilion. The blue and white color scheme offers a subtle, mutable canvas; the cornflower-blue alpaca curtains, powder-blue linen sofas, and white-painted chairs with gold upholstery are the epitome of classical understatement in the living room. Art brings texture and moments of calm—no distraction from the fog-infused panorama. "I told Greg I wanted to go back to my roots, with Gustavian tones and my favorite family antiques," says the homeowner. "Thanks to his polished design, the past and the present come together perfectly."

OPPOSITE PAGE: *A Gustavian console and modern painting provide a shapely counterpoint to the sleek mirrored wall.* FOLLOWING PAGES: *Silvery-blue upholstery shimmers in the living room's soft gray light.*

OPPOSITE PAGE: *White-lacquered wall panels are a beguiling backdrop for a 17th-century Italian pilaster—and offer secret storage.* THIS PAGE: *An heirloom collection of Chinese export porcelain pops against cornflower-blue shelves.* FOLLOWING PAGES: *The Swedish palette is evident in the ample bedroom, which pairs the requisite powder-blue curtains with glamorous tawny pillows.*

ALABASTER/ALMO
BISQUE/BONE/BU
CASHMERE/CELAD
COTTON/CREAM
ECRU/FEATHER
FROST/GRANITE
HEAVEN/HYDRAN
LACE/LINEN/MAP
NICKEL/NOISETT
OPAL/OYSTER/PA
PEBBLE/SHADO
SMOKE/SWAN/TAU

ND/BEIGE/BISCUIT
FF/CAPPUCCINIO
ON/CHALK/
/EAU DE NIL
FLAX/FOAM/
GRAPHITE/GRIS
GEA/ICICLE/
E/MILK/MINERAL
E/OATMEAL/ONYX
CHMENT/PEARL
W/SHELL/SISAL
PE/TOAST/TOFFEE

Rich &

Robust

Vibrant color unlocks something within us. Even in the most refined settings, maximalist, allover color is wild and free, untamed and unfettered. For those who have never met a color they didn't like, the world opens up into a rainbow of possibilities—daring voyages into the color wheel, with bold hues that appear in the form of walls lacquered a vivid cobalt blue or from a liberal brushstroke of upholstery and accents in ebullient shades of fuchsia and violet. There's an intimate authenticity to these homes, whose boundless energy and charisma radiate off the walls. Because there is nothing staid about a room the color of an egg yolk, the same can often be said of the families to who live inside—and their decorators, too.

LONE STAR SPIRIT A new house in Dallas expertly merges classical French architecture, sublime antiques, and a vivid palette.

After living with her husband in a striking, all-neutral contemporary home in a secluded neighborhood in Dallas for more than twenty-five years, a widowed octogenarian decided it was high time to build the house she'd always wanted. With the help of her dear friend, the late Dallas decorator Beverly Field, she said goodbye to her modern manse, purchased a lot much closer to the heart of town, and found inspiration in the neoclassical limestone pavilions of 18th-century France.

The château-like home's luminous entrance hall alone features marble floors and a glossy, arched ceiling where antique Venetian mirrors, glass obelisks, and Swedish chairs shimmer in the light-drenched space. "I approach every room as a painting and balance it with color," said Field. Bold colors and patterns reign—she even lacquered the library red, much to the homeowner's delight. "It's the perfect blend of pomegranate and tomato that flatters everyone," she said. "And when you look great in a room, you feel great." The result is highly sophisticated eclecticism—and an exuberant house brimming with life, which has operated at full tilt with a steady stream of parties and events since move-in day. "I wanted to create a magic kingdom for my client, something elegant and glamorous without being pompous," said Field. "I paired all of the fabulous antiques with a dash of something new. It makes it all so much more interesting and personal."

209

OPPOSITE PAGE: *A guest bedroom's wild array of patterns is unified by a cohesive palette.*

THIS PAGE: *A quartet of 18th-century Marie Antoinette chairs hold court under a bold contemporary painting by Robert Zakanitch.* **OPPOSITE PAGE:** *A reflective wall accentuates the ornate shape of an Italian Rococo mirror; gilt-encrusted chairs are embellished with bright turquoise seatbacks.* **FOLLOWING PAGES:** *Vivid tomato-red lacquer paint sets off an eclectic display of books and antique porcelain.*

THIS PAGE: *A collection of 18th-century plates creates a whimsical tableau in a dining room the color of mint-chip ice cream.* **OPPOSITE PAGE:** *Italian 19th-century mirrors and a collection of blue-and-white porcelain punctuate a stately hallway.*

217

OPPOSITE PAGE: *The sleek kitchen, clad in aquamarine tiles, is illuminated by a modern, sculptural fixture.*
THIS PAGE: *A robin's-egg-blue morning room is a casual complement to the kitchen.* **FOLLOWING PAGES:** *In the master bedroom, a garden motif set against a bright blue background is echoed in the crystal chandelier.*

BRIGHTEN UP When a New York couple decided to banish the beige once and for all, they turned to a young Manhattan maestro of color for an immersive experience.

When decorator Nick Olsen first met with the young couple in their condominium on the Upper East Side, he was surprised to see how they were living: surrounded by beige and ivory. "It wasn't a reflection of who they are at all," says Olsen, who is known for his mastery of wild, whimsical color juxtapositions. "They are vivid and animated, and love to express themselves."

The couple, who has two young sons, had decided they were ready for a bit of glam. Still, they tiptoed into a full makeover by first asking Olsen to re-do a small den first. Once merely an afterthought, the room has become the centerpiece of the home, with walls lacquered ink blue and a huge abstract painting hanging over the midnight velvet sofa. "Everyone fights to be in there now," says the decorator.

After such resounding success, the couple gave Olsen the nod to transform the rest of the apartment while the family was away for the summer. It was a spectacular reveal when they arrived home in August, the subtle neutrals replaced by Olsen's daring combinations, like the many shades of gold and violet in the living and dining rooms or the peacock blue that enlivens the master bedroom. Like the couple, the space has a joyful element that feels theatrical: "They're like a new, fabulous version of Lucy and Ricky —very fiery and funny," says Olsen. "This seems like an ideal setting for them."

221

OPPOSITE PAGE: *Custom-painted geometrics reverberate on the floors and walls of the apartment's entry hall.*

"I like to lacquer the ceiling—as long as it hasn't been ruined by recessed lighting, that is! Especially in a modern space, the reflectivity adds a much-needed shimmer. At night, in dim lamplight, it feels super glamorous. And in the daytime, the lacquer amplifies the light in the room." — Nick Olsen

THIS PAGE: *The walls of the open living and dining room are covered in a reflective paper that Albert Hadley once used in one of the many famed incarnations of his own Manhattan apartment.*
OPPOSITE PAGE: *The expansive living area includes a bold violet velvet sofa and an elegant settee with electric pink ribbon tucked behind nailhead trim.*

OPPOSITE PAGE: *The jewel box of a den, suffused entirely in primary shades, was the first room Olsen tackled. The pale patchwork cowhide carpet brightens a room that might otherwise feel dark and balances the strong hues.* **THIS PAGE:** *Olsen upholstered dining chairs in a sunshine yellow leather. A neoclassical screen in Fromental wallpaper adds a dose of elegant, organic pattern.*

THIS PAGE: *Caramel-colored midcentury tub chairs and malachite-patterned side tables are a warm counterpoint to a bright cerulean settee.* **OPPOSITE PAGE:** *One of Olsen's favorite "moments" is the master bedroom, with kaleidoscopic paper, a custom metal birdcage bed, and peacock-blue silk-taffeta curtains.*

PRETTY GRAND An upper-crust Manhattan apartment brims with major decorating but retains a lively, lovely sense of fun.

In this spacious Beaux Arts apartment on Manhattan's Upper East Side, Nick Olsen drew out all the big guns of proper top-drawer decorating: taffeta curtains and lambrequins, tufted velvet upholstery, and hand-painted silk wall coverings. You'd think the resulting scheme would elicit excellent posture and perhaps the tiniest yawn—but you'd be wrong.

Instead, it's buoyant and enchanting, thanks to Olsen's exuberant yet disciplined color sense and his clever way of balancing a freewheeling range of patterns and furnishings. "There can't be too much matching going on," says Olsen. "I put a tomato-red French chair next to an oxblood porcelain garden seat, and you might say, 'Hmmm—that's a little off.' But there has to be something a little off in a room, or it will look overdecorated."

The whole apartment, in fact, operates according to this system of checks and balances. The foyer's olive curtains with tasseled fringe? They're not striped taffeta, but a vintage, slubby raw silk chosen for its easy drape and subdued shade. The master bedroom's new four-poster bed? It arrived in dark mahogany but Olsen gave it a white-painted finish to lighten it up. Throughout the apartment, he mixes ikats, animal prints, chintzes, florals, and geometrics—and while it's a lot to behold, somehow it's never too much. "It might look tossed off," he says, "but it's a delicate balance. I go to bed thinking about it."

229

OPPOSITE PAGE: *A leopard-print carpet provides instant glamour in a daffodil family room.*
FOLLOWING PAGES: *The 19th-century Italian console in the living room—covered in sky-blue paint and gilded relief ornament—is paired effortlessly with a 1940s-style green banquette in a rich olive velvet.*

THIS PAGE: *Pale blue pops against the white coffered ceiling's molding—and reappears in a sofa and on the walls in the entry.* **OPPOSITE PAGE:** *The clients' collection of old family portraits feel fresh in Olsen's hands.*

OPPOSITE PAGE: *An Empire valence isn't fussy when coupled with a boldly patterned floor and a hit of icy blue.* **THIS PAGE:** *Sinuously curved lambrequins transform standard windows in a dining room the color of chocolate milk.*

237

OPPOSITE PAGE: *A citron lamp provides continuity between the yellow family room and a serene master bedroom.* **THIS PAGE:** *City life is fresh and sunny with a hand-painted garden scene on the walls.*

A BRIGHT IDEA
When a young family trades SoHo for Park Avenue, they enlist Celerie Kemble to blend the best of both worlds.

"This was a downtown couple moving uptown with their family," says designer Celerie Kemble of a relocation considered positively suburban by the denizens of SoHo. "We didn't want them to get up here and feel uncool or unyoung." She points to a dazzling cornflower blue she chose for the dining room walls, part of the gut renovation of a three-bedroom apartment. "It's strong, but the couple has so much style, they can handle it."

A clue to her clients' bold taste came in their choice of provocative art, which adds a thrilling edge throughout the home. "We've always found it easy to express ourselves through our art," says the husband, "but our previous apartment was all taupes and grays. Celerie helped us pull our love for color into our everyday life. It makes our home very personal."

The fireworks begin in a foyer dramatically sheathed in oxblood grass cloth, a color that riffs on the dramatic tortoiseshell wallpaper inserted between the ceiling coffers. Furnishings with strong shapes and deep colors ground the living room; to help the couple unwind, Kemble cloaked the master bedroom in a luminous silk paper and soft, watery blues.

"This apartment is about the truth of things for a young family," Kemble says. "They wanted their home to have a certain amount of order, which it does, but at some point, you realize that life is colorful mayhem. And that's the fun."

239

OPPOSITE PAGE: *Kemble's clients love it when guests are shocked to see such a theatrical, richly hued entry in an Upper East Side apartment.* **FOLLOWING PAGES:** *With space at a premium, the dramatic cobalt dining room doubles as a library.*

245

ISN'T IT ROMANTIC
With a rich, painterly palette, Miles Redd transforms a Manhattan apartment into a welcoming home with a dazzling disposition.

Designer Miles Redd is living proof that the magic truly is in the mix. "If I showed you a sample of that taxicab-yellow lacquer, you might think it looked like shellacked dried egg yolk," he says, referring to the living room walls of an Upper West Side apartment he decorated for a couple with four young children. "But if you put it with blues and greens, soft grays and reds, it gives you the feeling of brandy held up to the firelight instead."

The Georgia-born, New York–based wunderkind is known for his irreverent slant on high style. Deep hues and dramatic flourishes imbue rooms with old-world charm and comfort. The palette is surprisingly primary: reds, yellows, and shades of blue anchor each room, creating a cohesive color experience. The gold and scarlet dashes in the otherwise pale blue-and-grisaille wallpaper of the prewar apartment's entrance hall recur in the living room's glowing walls, crimson leather–covered dining chairs and silk lampshades, and Redd's signature upholstered leather doors; the wallpaper's sky reappears as soft blue curtains framing views of Central Park, a deep cerulean in the study, and an ethereal Gracie-papered bedroom. But matching, in the most traditional sense of the word, is entirely optional in Redd's playbook: "There's nothing yellow in the living room except those walls," he explains, "but when the wall color is so strong, everything fades, pops, or feels soft against it. When you go bold with primary shades, they work with everything."

249

OPPOSITE PAGE: *Upholstered doors, clad in scarlet leather and nailhead trim, lead into the effervescent living room.* **FOLLOWING PAGES:** *A colorful Sultanabad rug inspired the living room's sensational palette.*

Sorolla THE MASTERWORKS

COROT

John Singer Sargent THE EARLY PORTRAITS

Anders Zorn

HUMAN ANATOMY FOR ARTISTS · ELIOT

VREELAND MEMOS

SULTAN

"Upholstered doors have become a signature of mine. I love them because I think they are often such a missed opportunity—there's a real tendency to just slap up a six-paneled door and call it a day, but they can make such a statement and become a part of the decoration." —Miles Redd

OPPOSITE PAGE: *A cheerful stripe enlivens a 19th-century English cabinet.*
THIS PAGE: *Deep hues and dramatic flourishes imbue an apartment with old-world charm and comfort.*

THIS PAGE: *The informal dining room embraces old and new, pairing Louis XV chairs with a marble-topped Saarinen dining table and a plaster chandelier.* **OPPOSITE PAGE:** *With its grisaille wall covering and old-world furnishings, the stately entry hall is a study in modern elegance.*

OPPOSITE PAGE: *The master bedroom is layered with varying fabrics united by the color blue.*
THIS PAGE: *Ladylike fringe trims a velvet sofa in the plush cerulean study.*

YOU'RE INVITED At a historic Atlanta estate, Miles Redd marries high-style living with 21st-century ease and elegance.

Surrounded by rills, espaliered fruit trees, and terraced gardens, Boxwood is an illustrious 1920s property designed by the eminent Atlanta architect Philip Shutze and sited on five exquisitely-groomed acres in the middle of Buckhead. When a young family moved into the storied estate, they called on Redd to imbue the home with old-fashioned opulence. "They were looking for a high-flying glamour that reflected the spirit the house was built in," says Redd, who grew up in Atlanta and had ogled the estate since childhood. "There's a fifties sensibility to it, with nods to Babe Paley, Brooke Astor, and the Duchess of Windsor. We were definitely looking back in time to look forward."

Redd suffused the house with romance and femininity. Color is liberally yet elegantly deployed—primarily shades of rich blue. A cheerful tented breakfast room is done up in a jaunty aqua-and-ivory stripe. "It's like a pavilion off the kitchen," says Redd. "It feels like a vacation." The plush living room's walls were covered in a peacock-blue satin, and the adjoining service bar's walls, cabinets, and ceiling are lacquered an intense turquoise. Taking inspiration from the overhead mural in New York's Grand Central Terminal, Redd enlivened the service bar's vaulted ceiling with constellations corresponding to the family's zodiac signs. "Blue is the warmest color," says Redd with a laugh. "There's just no shade that doesn't delight and excite me."

259

OPPOSITE PAGE: *The Bird Room's pattern is a restored painted Chinese wallpaper. Redd deploys leopard and tiger print— here on tiger velvet slipper chairs—as though they were neutrals.* **FOLLOWING PAGES:** *Plush yet relaxed, the living room can seat forty without getting noisy, thanks to an antique Oushak carpet and walls upholstered in silk satin.*

OPPOSITE PAGE: *A small room gets an extra punch when trim, walls, and ceiling are saturated in blue.* **THIS PAGE:** *The ebulliently striped walls in the tented breakfast room were laminated to protect them from the sticky fingers of the family's children.* **FOLLOWING PAGES:** *The opulent master bedroom is an ode to old-school, high-style decorating with voluptuous silk curtains trimmed in ruffles, a leopard print carpet, and a matching dog bed.*

COLOR BALANCE With more than a hint of tint, a new palette energizes a Dallas house.

Leave it to a Texan to turn tradition on its head. Designer Julie Hayes transformed a 1980s white-columned Greek Revival house with quiet interiors into a vibrant residence for a Dallas family. Her fearless palette injected energy into spaces that might typically be sedate—playful yet elegant rooms humming with unexpected details. "We wanted the décor to have a collected feel," says Hayes.

The vibrant living room sets the tone, lacquered in a hue somewhere between an intense apple green and a deep avocado. "I didn't want something expected," says Hayes. "I like colors that are off by one or two shades." Metallics play a big role in the décor, too. In the formal dining room, Hayes played off the gentle glow of the hand-painted Gracie wallpaper installed by the previous owners, covered the chairs in another shade of silver, and replaced old wainscoting with antiqued mirrored glass. "I wanted it to look pretty at night," Hayes says. "The whole room shimmers."

Perhaps the most unusual highlight of the house is the kitchen, with its bright citron-colored cabinets topped off with an ornately plastered, barrel-vaulted, lavender ceiling. The contrast catches you off guard—in a good way. "People live in their kitchens, so why not make it fabulous?" Hayes says. "The architect and I added the Robert Adam–inspired neoclassical plaster ceiling, which is an element of surprise here but also appropriate to the house. It's a classic house with a fresh effect."

267

OPPOSITE PAGE: *Fearless color makes for a playful but elegant kitchen.* FOLLOWING PAGES: *Yellow chairs create continuity in a chocolate-hued family room off the kitchen.*

271

OPPOSITE PAGE: *The wallpaper's sheen inspired Hayes to add reflective surfaces: chairs in patent leather and a silver fabric, a high-gloss table, and a mirrored pedestal.* **THIS PAGE:** *Hayes upholstered the sofas using the shinier reverse side of the fabric to inject more drama in the avocado-colored living room.* **FOLLOWING PAGES:** *A bedroom is a riot of red-and-white patterns.*

A SENSE OF PLAY Irreverence marks a vibrant, ever-changing Parisian pied-à-terre.

Argentine designer Roberto Bergero is a hands-on practitioner, unafraid to climb a ladder to embellish his own parlor with Velázquez-inspired frescoes, forge his own plaster chandeliers, sew flowing taffeta curtains, build a miniature four-poster bed for his dog, paint canvas rugs—or anything else that might contribute to a certain *art de vivre*. He splits his time between a house in Buenos Aires and this Parisian pied-à-terre, where he updates, renovates, and refreshes his surroundings at an alarming rate. It's not uncommon to visit his home one week for dinner and find it bursting with Baroque objects and furniture—only to pop back a week later to discover a Directoire setting replete with Gustavian sofas and daybeds. "I treat interiors as if they were stage sets," he says.

His multidisciplinary talents are on display in this incarnation of his flat. Recovering from what he called "a serious 18th-century phase," Bergero repainted formerly monochrome Versailles-gray walls a vivid Tyrrhenian pink and set them off with apple-green plaster medallions he made himself, along with neoclassical busts and coral branch sconces. There are 1940s chauffeuse chairs covered in cherry-colored satin and Directoire sofas in black-and-white stripes.

It adds up to an expressive, colorful residence steeped in all of the volatility and vitality of its owner—and unpredictability is part of his charm. "It's a decorator's privilege," he says. Today, he prefers strong colors instead of a dull palette, but one never knows what tomorrow will bring.

OPPOSITE PAGE: *Bold pastel colorations are offset by heavy doses of white trim.*

THIS PAGE: *Artful configurations and handmade touches enliven a Paris flat.* OPPOSITE PAGE: *A black-and-white stripe adds a contrasting note against a sea of solid fabrics and paints.*

OPPOSITE PAGE: *The sun shining through yellow silk casts a warm glow.* **THIS PAGE:** *The dining room is a play on vivid contrasts; a hot-pink screen is a quick shot of additional color in a vibrant room.*

AMBER AMETHYST
BUTTERSCOTCH
CERISE CERULE
CITRON COBALT C
JADE LAVENDER
MALACHITE MANG
ORCHID OXBL
PERIWINKLE PE
POINSETTIA POMB
SALMON SEPIA S
VERMILION WALN
WENGE WINE W

APPLE AVOCADO
CANARY CAYENNE
AN CINNAMON
RIMSON EMERALD
MAGENTA MAIZE
O MYRTLE OCHRE
OOD PERIDOT
RSIMMON PLUM
GRANATE RUSSET
UNFLOWER TEAL
UT WATERMELON
NTERGREEN ZINC

ACKNOWLEDGMENTS

Many, many, many people are involved in the production and creation of a book, and there are plenty of folks to thank for their support and contributions to this endeavor, as well as to *Veranda*. My sincerest appreciation to:

The staff of editors at *Veranda* and the Hearst Design Group, for their continued passion for all things beautiful.

Carolyn Englefield, who has produced and styled most of the homes in this book. Her exquisite, unerring eye always captures the warmth and grace that defines *Veranda*.

Suzanne Noli, for interpreting my vision for this book into the one that you hold in your hands.

Kaitlin Petersen, for contributing new text that's informative and inspiring, and for adapting the original articles.

Jacqueline Deval, for her commitment to publishing this book and her thoughtful consideration of the *Veranda* brand.

Chris Thompson and the team at Sterling Publishing, for their guidance, patience, and expertise.

Joanna Coles and Newell Turner, for their ongoing support of *Veranda*.

The writers, whose gracious prose reflects the easy elegance of the *Veranda* lifestyle.

The photographers, whose brilliant images help define the magazine issue after issue.

The architects and designers who entrust us with their projects, as well as the homeowners who open their doors to us.

PHOTOGRAPHY CREDITS

FRONT COVER Photography © Max Kim-Bee
BACK COVER Photography © Antoine Bootz
AUTHOR PHOTO Photography © Erica George Dines

PAGE 2 Photography © Max Kim-Bee, interior design by Kelli Ford and Kirsten Fitzgibbons, architecture by Larry E. Boerder, produced by Carolyn Englefield

PAGE 4 Photography © Simon Upton, interior design by Suzanne Kasler, architechture by Heather Francis Robers

PAGE 6 Photography © Mali Azima, interior design by Kay Douglass, architechture by Philip Trammell Shutze, produced by Lisa Newsom Rascoe

PAGES 8, 82, 204 Photography © Richard Prince

PAGE 138 Photography © Alison Gootee, produced by Melissa Colgan

ISLAND IDYLL
PAGES 12–21 Photography © William Waldron, interior design by Ruthie Sommers, produced by Carolyn Englefield

FOR THE LOVE OF CHIC
PAGES 22–27 Photography © Franchesco Lagnese, interior design by Ruthie Sommers, produced by Victoria Jones

HAUTE HUES
PAGES 28–37 Photography © Max Kim-Bee, interior design by Kelli Ford and Kirsten Fitzgibbons, architecture by Larry E. Boerder, landscape architecture by Paul Fields, produced by Carolyn Englefield

ENDLESS SUMMER
PAGES 38–45 Photography © Melanie Acevedo, interior design by Kelli Ford and Kirsten Fitzgibbons, produced by Carolyn Englefield

NATURAL INSTINCT
PAGES 46–55 Photography © Victoria Pearson, interior design by Jan Showers, produced by David M. Murphy

EASY DOES IT
PAGES 56–63 Photography © Max Kim-Bee, interior design by Amanda Nisbet, architecture by Stuart L. Disston, landscape design by Bradford Kent Spaulding, produced by Carolyn Englefield

A DELFT TOUCH
PAGES 64–71 Photography © James Merrell, interior design by Cathy Kincaid, produced by David M. Murphy

HIGH VOLTAGE
PAGES 72–79 Photography © Bjorn Wallander, interior design by Alessandra Branca, produced by Carolyn Englefield

MAGICAL MOOD
PAGES 86–95 Photography © Erica George Dines, interior design by Susan Ferrier, architecture by Jonathan Torode

A SOFT TOUCH
PAGES 96–103 Photography © Erica George Dines, interior design by Susan Ferrier, architecture by Bobby McAlpine and Greg Tankersley

PURPLE REIGN
PAGES 104–111 Photography © Simon Utpon, interior design by Suzanne Kasler, architecture by Heather Francis Robers

PERSONAL BEST
PAGES 112–119 Photography © Annie Schlechter, interior design by Jane Hawkins Hoke, architecture by James Carter, landscape design by Norman Kent Johnson, produced by David M. Murphy

INDEX

NOTE: Page references in *italics* indicate/include photographs and refer to location of photo captions.

HEARSTBOOKS

An Imprint of Sterling Publishing
1166 Avenue of the Americas

VERANDA is a registered trademark of Hearst Communications, Inc.

© 2017 by Hearst Communications, Inc.

ISBN 978-1-61837-232-1

Distributed in Canada by Sterling Publishing Co., Inc.
c/o Canadian Manda Group, 664 Annette Street
Toronto, Ontario, Canada M6S 2C8
Distributed in the United Kingdom by GMC Distribution Services
Castle Place, 166 High Street, Lewes, East Sussex, England BN7 1XU
Distributed in Australia by NewSouth Books
45 Beach Street, Coogee, NSW 2034, Australia

For information about custom editions, special sales, and premium and
corporate purchases, please contact Sterling Special Sales at 800-805-5489
or specialsales@sterlingpublishing.com.

Manufactured in China

2 4 6 8 10 9 7 5 3 1

www.sterlingpublishing.com

Jacket design by Scott Russo
Interior design by Suzanne Noli and Sharon Jacobs